Lions and Tigers and Leopards
THE BIG CATS

A Bengal tiger cools off with a swim.

by Jennifer C. Urquhart

BOOKS FOR YOUNG EXPLORERS
NATIONAL GEOGRAPHIC SOCIETY

Copyright © 1990 National Geographic Society   Library of Congress CIP Data: p. 32

TIGERS

Tigers live in Siberia and in other parts of Asia.

Three tiger cubs are curious. Can you guess what they see? Maybe it is something to play with. Maybe it is their mother coming to feed them.

It is bath time for this Bengal tiger cub. The mother licks the cub to clean it. She protects her cubs until they are almost two years old. She teaches them how to hunt. Then they will leave and be on their own

A Siberian tiger catches a fish to eat. Unlike many other kinds of cats, tigers like water. They swim in it and find food there. The tiger will need a lot more than one little fish to eat! Siberian tigers are the largest cats in the world. Some weigh as much as 14 first graders all together!

LIONS

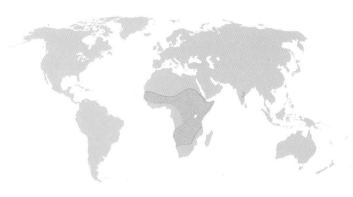

Lions live in parts of Africa and in one forest in India.

My, what big teeth you have! Long front teeth help a lion kill prey for food. He cuts the meat with his back teeth. He uses his rough tongue to clean his fur. Only the male lion has a furry mane on his head and neck.

Is this lion roaring, or is he just yawning? Most big cats can roar, but lions roar more than other kinds do. Roaring helps them tell other lions to keep out of their territory, where they live and hunt.

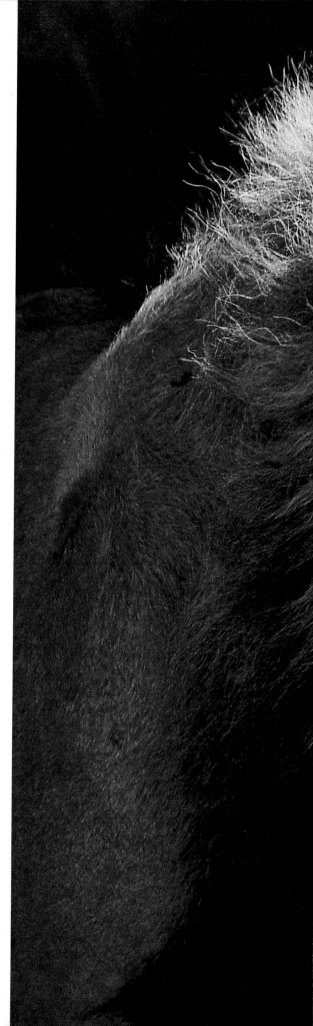

A female lion, called a lioness, cuddles a cub. Another lioness carries her cub gently in her mouth. Spots on the cubs help hide them from enemies. The spots will disappear when the cubs are grown up.

Lions live together in families called prides. The lionesses take care of all the cubs together, even ones that are not their own.

A male lion comes near a rhinoceros. What do you think the lion will do? The sharp horns of the rhinoceros are dangerous. These big animals usually avoid each other. Lions eat smaller animals like zebras and antelopes. The females do most of the hunting for the pride. This lioness is creeping toward her prey. She is ready to leap.

LEOPARDS

A leopard rests in a tree on a hot day. At night, it comes down to hunt for food. It will drag its prey up a tree and eat it there so other animals cannot steal it.

Leopards usually live alone or travel in small groups.

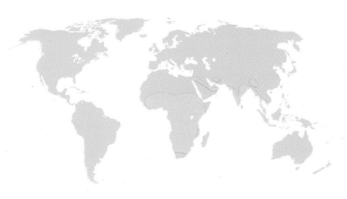

Leopards live in parts of Africa, the Middle East, and Asia.

A leopard cub climbs a tree. Another cub hangs between two branches. Maybe they are practicing to be good climbers! Leopards spend a lot of time in trees.

An adult leopard crouches to sip some water. Then it may hunt for food. These cats are good hunters. They can move very quietly. Spots on their fur blend with trees and grass and help camouflage them when they stalk prey.

JAGUARS

Jaguars live in parts of Mexico, and south through Argentina.

Both of these big cats are jaguars, even though one is almost black and the other is spotted. If you look very carefully, you can see some spots on the dark jaguar. A few leopards also have dark coats.

Do you think that the light-colored jaguar looks like a leopard? The jaguar's spots have black dots in the middle. A leopard's spots do not.

MOUNTAIN LIONS

Mountain lions live in parts of North America,
and south through Chile.

A mountain lion and a black bear
have surprised each other.
What do you think will happen next?

This kind of cat has other names, too.
Sometimes it is called a cougar, or
a puma. Mountain lions are very shy.
They avoid most other animals.
This bear and mountain lion only met
by chance. They will probably leave
before either one gets hurt.

A mountain lion lies in a pool of water to stay cool. Two others find shade from the sun in a cave. These cats often live in hot, dry places.

Sometimes baby mountain lions, called kittens, stay in caves while their mother hunts for food for them. This kitten is sharpening its claws on a piece of wood. Have you ever seen a pet cat do the same thing?

CHEETAHS

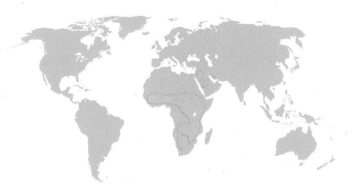

Cheetahs live in parts of Africa and the Middle East.

Two cheetahs in Africa are hunting for a meal. They stalk, creeping very slowly toward their prey, probably a gazelle or an impala. If the animal seems frightened, the cheetahs "freeze," or stand very still. Then they move ahead again.

A mother cheetah hides her cubs in the high grass or under a bush while she hunts. Cheetahs hunt in open grasslands. Unlike most other big cats, they stalk during the day.

See how the cheetah stretches out when it runs after its prey! Over a short distance, cheetahs run faster than any other animal that lives on land. They can move as fast as a car travels on a highway. Because cheetahs are not as large or as strong as other big cats, they depend on speed to catch prey.

Cheetah cubs play-fight. Playing like this help them learn skills they will need later to hunt. A mother nurses her cubs in the grass. Do you think they are purring? Unlike most big cats, cheetahs can purr.

Cheetahs do not roar like other big cats. The mothers make a chirping noise, like a bird, to call their babies. Cheetah cubs have a mane of silvery-gray hair. Perhaps the hair protects them from the weather. Or maybe it helps hide them from other animals that might attack when their mother goes away to find food.

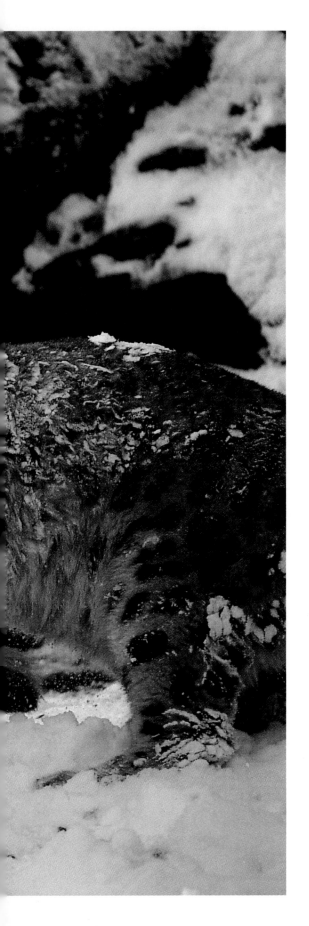

SNOW LEOPARDS

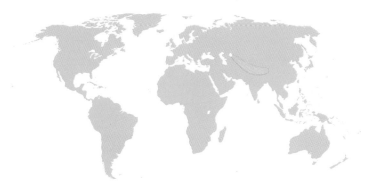

Snow leopards live in high-mountain areas of central Asia.

Swat, swat! A snow leopard cub bats at another cub. They are playing in the snow. Snow leopards live in the mountains, where it snows a lot. Thick hair on their paws helps them walk on top of the deep snow.

In summer, snow leopards follow their prey higher in the mountains. Their gray-colored fur blends with the rocks. These cats can leap long distances when they are chasing their prey.

Snow leopard cubs snuggle together. Snow leopards have thick, woolly fur to keep them warm in winter. Mother snow leopards put some of their own fur in their dens to help keep the babies warm. Do you think these cubs look ready for sleep?

Published by
The National Geographic Society, Washington, D.C.
Gilbert M. Grosvenor, *President and Chairman of the Board*
Melvin M. Payne, Thomas W. McKnew, *Chairmen Emeritus*
Owen R. Anderson, *Executive Vice President*
Robert L. Breeden, *Senior Vice President, Publications
    and Educational Media*

Prepared by
The Special Publications and School Services Division
Donald J. Crump, *Director*
Philip B. Silcott, *Associate Director*
Bonnie S. Lawrence, *Assistant Director*

Staff for this book
Jane H. Buxton, *Managing Editor*
Charles E. Herron, *Illustrations Editor*
Jody Bolt, *Art Director*
Gail N. Hawkins, *Researcher*
Artemis S. Lampathakis, *Illustrations Assistant*
Carol R. Curtis, Lisa A. LaFuria, Sandra F. Lotterman,
    Katy Old, Dru McLoud Stancampiano, Marilyn Williams,
    Staff Assistants

Engraving, Printing, and Product Manufacture
George V. White, *Director,* and Vincent P. Ryan, *Manager,
    Manufacturing and Quality Management*
David V. Showers, *Production Manager*
Lewis R. Bassford, *Production Project Manager*

Consultants
William A. Xanten, Jr., National Zoological Park,
    Smithsonian Institution, *Scientific Consultant*
Sue Appleby Purcell, *Educational Consultant*
Dr. Lynda Bush, *Reading Consultant*

Illustrations Credits
Gerard Lacz/PETER ARNOLD, INC. (cover, 2-3);
ANIMALS ANIMALS/Zig Leszczynski (1);
Alan and Sandy Carey (2); Tom McHugh/
PHOTO RESEARCHERS, INC. (4-5, 16); Boyd Norton (6-7);
Günter Ziesler/PETER ARNOLD, INC. (8);
Mitch Reardon/PHOTO RESEARCHERS, INC. (8-9);
Steven J. Krasemann/DRK PHOTO (10-11 all);
Anup Shah-OKAPIA 1989/PHOTO RESEARCHERS, INC. (12-13);
E.R. Degginger (13, 18-19); Lex Hes (14-15 all);
Alan Carey/PHOTO RESEARCHERS, INC. (16-17);
ANIMALS ANIMALS/Leonard Lee Rue III (20-21);
Wolfgang Bayer/BRUCE COLEMAN INC. (21 upper);
ANIMALS ANIMALS/Charles Palek (21 right);
Len Rue, Jr. (22-23); David Weintraub/ALLSTOCK, INC. (24-25);
ANIMALS ANIMALS/Anup Shah, Manoj Shah (26, 32);
Gregory G. Dimijian, M.D./ (26-27);
ANIMALS ANIMALS/Michael Dick (28-29, 30-31).

Library of Congress ⊂⋿ Data
Urquhart, Jennifer C.
    Lions and tigers and leopards : the big cats / by Jennifer C. Urquhart.
    p. cm. — (Books for young explorers)
    Includes bibliographical references.
    Summary: Text and pictures introduce lions, tigers, leopards, and the other big cats.
    ISBN 0-87044-820-X (regular edition). — ISBN 0-87044-825-0 (library edition).
    1. Panthera—Juvenile literature. 2. Lions—Juvenile literature. 3. Tigers—Juvenile
literature. 4. Leopard—Juvenile literature. [1. Lions. 2. Tigers. 3. Leopard.]
I. Title. II. Title: Big cats. III. Series.
QL737.C23U77 1990
599.74'428—dc20   90—6481
                                                    ⊂⋿
                                                    AC

A Bengal tiger spots something ahead. Her cub sees you! Their stripes and the markings on their faces are different. They are like fingerprints. Every tiger in the whole world has markings different from all the rest.

Cover: A mother tiger relaxes with her playful cubs.

More About

**Lions and Tigers
and Leopards**

THE BIG CATS

Whether striped or spotted, marbled or plain, whether a small pet cat or a giant Siberian tiger (4-5)*, members of the cat family have much in common. With rare exceptions, cats have retractable claws. They have highly developed night vision as well as whiskers that help guide them. Raspy tongues help them groom and eat. A tiger-striped pet feline displays the same tactics in hunting a mouse as his wild tiger cousin uses to bring down a deer. Both hunt alone. They stalk silently, then pounce suddenly to kill the prey, usually by suffocation.

Scientists generally put cats in two groups: the small cats and the big cats. The so-called big cats in this book usually roar rather than purr. They eat lying down rather than crouched. They rest with their tails straight out rather than curled around themselves. Their eyes differ from those of small cats. But these classifications are not abso-

lute. The mountain lion (18-21), for instance, though as large as a leopard (12-15), is often classified with the small cats. Though small, the snow leopard (28-31) has characteristics usually associated with big cats. And the cheetah (22-27) has variations unique to its species.

In their natural habitats—forests and savannas of Africa, of the Americas, and of other regions of the world—big cats play an important role at the top of the food chain. By hunting, they help balance populations of large herd animals, such as wildebeests, zebras, antelopes, and deer, as well as small animals such as rabbits and mice.

The survival of many of the large cats is in jeopardy. For generations, hunters targeted them for their fur. Laws now protect many of them, but new threats have arisen. As carnivorous hunters, big cats need large areas to roam

*Numbers in parentheses refer to pages in *Lions and Tigers and Leopards: The Big Cats*.

LEN RUE, JR.

Who watches whom? With fearless grace, a cheetah climbs a tourist vehicle in East Africa. Remnant populations of the big cats survive in remote regions or in parks and reserves where visitors can observe them.

ROW 1: KENNETH W. FINK/BRUCE COLEMAN INC.; GEORGE CALEF/MASTERFILE; JOE McDONALD/BRUCE COLEMAN INC.; TOM McHUGH/PHOTO RESEARCHERS, INC.
ROW 2: W. PERRY CONWAY; LEX HES; GREGORY G. DIMIJIAN, M.D.; GALEN ROWELL/MOUNTAIN LIGHT

Can you guess each cat from its portrait? Numbered clues will help you. (Answers below.)
1. Great tree climber, sometimes spotted, sometimes dark. 2. King of the roarers. 3. Speed champion.
4. Sometimes spotted, inhabitant of the forests of the Americas. 5. Shy cat of the Americas. 6. See number one.
7. Largest of the big cats. Rarely has whitish coat. 8. Inhabits snowy mountain peaks.

Answers: 1. Leopard 2. Lion 3. Cheetah 4. Jaguar 5. Mountain lion 6. Leopard 7. Tiger (white variant) 8. Snow leopard

in search of prey. With human populations burgeoning, forests and grasslands are rapidly shrinking.

In Africa game preserves and parks have helped protect territory for many of the great cats. These parks draw tourists and bring income to the various countries. But the pressure of visitors can be detrimental, particularly to cheetahs. They usually hunt alone. Though capable of great speed, cheetahs often miss their target. They are smaller and not as strong as other large cats and are therefore more likely to lose their prey to other animals. Because cheetahs often hunt during the day, tourist vans can interfere by destroying the element of surprise. Efforts in India to save tigers are meeting with success. From about 40,000 less than a century ago, Bengal tigers (cover, 1-3, 32) dropped to about 1,800. Setting up reserves brought that number back to about 4,000 by 1989. The struggle to balance the needs of people with those of the big cats continues.

For fun closer to home, observe a pet cat. Much of its behavior is similar to that of the big cats in this book. Ball up some paper and tie a string around it. Drag the ball in front of the cat. See how it stalks and pounces. It may attack the paper with its claws extended. Watch the cat lick its paw, then use it like a washcloth to clean its face. Imagine that it is one of the big cats living in the wild.

Additional Reading

Serengeti Cats, by Joel and Alice Schick. (Philadelphia, Lippincott, 1977). Ages 9 and up.

Snow Leopard, ill. by Lynne Cherry. (New York, E. P. Dutton, 1987). Beginning readers.

Wild Cats, by Peggy D. Winston. (Washington, D.C., National Geographic Society, 1981). Ages 4-8.